3D (DDD)— DIMENSION DISCOVERY DIVISION

3D (DDD)—DIMENSION DISCOVERY DIVISION

RICHES WITHIN YOUR REACH
MONEY—CODE—DECODING

Saru Gwata

To order additional copies of this book, contact:
Xlibris
UK TFN: 0800 0148620 (Toll Free inside the UK)
UK Local: 02036 956328 (+44 20 3695 6328 from outside the UK)
www.Xlibrispublishing.co.uk
Orders@Xlibrispublishing.co.uk
825197

Contents

Preface

What inspired me to write this book is the knowledge I gained through reading books written by some great writers like Napoleon Hill and listening to motivational speakers like Bob Proctor and a good number of preachers of the Gospel, not to mention names. I got a lot of teaching in video forms and audio forms. I also get a good amount of useful information by watching useful teaching materials on TV and some documentaries. The Bible is my great source of inspiration and the greatest motivational book of all the books I have read. I happen to be a strong believer of the Word of God. You don't have to be one, but it's an added advantage if you are. My husband, Livingstone Gadwell, published his first book in the year 2020 and that really inspired me to write my own. He encouraged me to write my own.

Introduction

To make it easier to understand how you can get your hands on the RICHES WITHIN YOUR REACH, I will refer to two characters and how they lived their lives in different ways. If you follow closely when I explain the lives of these two people, you will find it easier to understand the 3D (DIMENSION DISCOVERY DIVISION) and the MONEY CODE.

Which group of people can benefit from reading this book?

You will understand how to prosper using that which you already possess but maybe, do not understand how to use. The illustrations are simplified for all diversities of culture to understand and to benefit from.

The words of wisdom shared in this book can benefit ANYONE—educated or uneducated, rich or poor, Christian or non-Christian, and regardless of gender, race, colour, or creed.

CHAPTER 1

HOW TO MAXIMISE YOUR POTENTIALS

To maximise your potentials, you have to be able to live above the five senses. How can one live above the five senses? You may want to ask. It is surely possible, though it takes a lot of determination and willpower. I will explain this in detail.

LIVING ABOVE THE FIVE SENSES

It has been discovered that you can live above the elements of this world and be able to achieve almost anything you want in this world. It is by maximising the potentials invested in your mind. You can achieve this by living above the five senses and entering into a DIMENSION above your five senses. I will give an illustration using TV Display Formats to make it easier to grasp the concept from the very beginning before we go deeper into the subject.

TELEVISION DISPLAY FORMATS / MAXIMISING YOUR POTENTIALS

Here's an illustration using TV DISPLAY FORMATS. Let us look at the HD (high-definition) TV format first. The HDTV has digital broadcasting that has better picture and sound quality than the standard-definition SDTV which has a lower digital resolution. Long before colour TV came into use, all TVs used to have black and white pictures. Things changed over the years to colour with SDTV and HDTV.

This explanation of TVs, is the same as the pathway of the life people live today. There are people today whose life is like a black-and-white TV, all dark, gloomy, blurry, uncertain, and not a well-defined pathway. This group of people do not know whether they are going or coming. They are not able to see clearly the direction of their lives. It is like groping in the dark in the hope of finding something somewhere. These people live unhappy lives and are usually not well educated. They are often drawn into crime, drugs, binge drinking, promiscuity, joblessness, wickedness, craftiness to get rich quick, and other unwanted things.

The group of people whose life is like the SDTV are the people who are usually educated, have good jobs and seemingly happy families, and manage a holiday or so a year. Despite all this, these people live average or just above-average lives. They usually get a salary that's enough for food, paying their bills, and very basic life commodities. Most of them are not contented with their lives. To get what they want in life, they have to put effort or struggle to get there but never really get there. The first character I will give reference to falls into this group, and her name is called Ruby Saunders.

The second group of people I will make reference are those who are like the HDTV. The second character I will make reference to falls into this group of people, and his name is Trey Thomas. Unfortunately, there is a very small percentage of people who belong to this group. I call this group the 3D—DIMENSION DISCOVERY DIVISION. Why? Because it is the discovery of the money code and the decoding of it. How? This will be explained later. You need to follow closely so you don't miss the key elements to unveil the riches that lie dormant somewhere inside you. It does not mean that all rich people live in this dimension, but one thing is certain, that you cannot live in this dimension and be poor.

It is a choice you have to make to be able to live and think above the five senses so as to MAXIMISE YOUR POTENTIALS and live a high-profile life or HIGH-DEFINITION life. You can live this high-definition life if you follow what is explained in this book step by step and do likewise. However, it requires a high level of discipline and focus.

THE TWO CHARACTERS

The two main characters I will make reference to throughout this book fall into the two TV format groups, that is, the SDTV and the HDTV group of people as explained earlier. The first character I will explain is called Ruby Saunders. She falls into the SDTV group. The second character I will explain is called Trey Thomas, who falls into the HDTV group.

UNCOVER THE POTENTIALS THAT LIE DORMANT IN YOUR MIND

First of all, you are going to discover what your mind can do for you. It looks like playing mind games, but it is not.

You are going to activate the potential in your mind that you never thought possible or even existed. This will give your life a turn around for a happier and more fulfilling life. In other words, you will be able to control the affairs of your life by utilising the 3D, which lies covertly in your mind.

I will use the Bible often as reference because I also discovered that all principles of success used by people who have made a difference in this life and in the life past are all based on Bible verses. Whether you believe in the Bible or not, it will work for you the same because it is a principle.

Before I explain to you the 3D, or DDD, which stands for DIMENSION DISCOVERY DIVISION. Unlike 3D, commonly known as the three dimension in the physical environment, this is not what I am referring to. I will base the explanation of this by sharing the lives of the two people as mentioned above, Ruby Saunders and Trey Thomas. These two characters are fictitious, they don't exist in real life, past or present. Some of the information is based on true life events and facts, which influenced many different people in different parts of the world at different intervals. Most of the information and events have been altered to protect the people's identities.

THE LIVES OF RUBY SAUNDERS AND TREY THOMAS

Trey Thomas is a male, while Ruby Saunders is a female. These two characters are of the same age group who lived in different towns in the same country, Zimbabwe. Trey lived in a town called Harare, the capital city, while Ruby lived in Bulawayo, the second-largest city in the country. These towns are 439.3 kilometres/272.9 miles apart and about a six-hour drive.

Trey and Ruby were at the same school and the same class in Harare when they completed their General Certificate of Education (GCE O-Level) as teenagers. They went different ways thereafter. Ruby passed this level of education with distinctions, while Trey did not make it; he dropped off school at this level.

RUBY'S LIFE EXPLAINED

Let us have a look at Ruby's life first, then after that, we will also look at Trey's life. This will help you understand what I will explain later. Ruby was always at the top of the class, from primary education to secondary education and tertiary education. She was known as an intelligent student short of genius.

As explained earlier, Ruby passed secondary education O-Level with distinctions, and that was when they went separate ways with Trey, her classmate. Ruby went further with education and obtained A-Level (Advanced Level) passes. She completed this level after two years of studies. This qualified her for higher education institutes. Her interest was in in the medical field so she enrolled at the University of Bulawayo and studied MEDICINE. Ruby successfully completed the six years training for a degree in medicine. After which she worked one year as a (Registrar- term used for junior doctors or medical graduates) to gain experience. She qualified the title Medical Doctor which in short I will refer as Dr.

In pursue of further studies in the medical field Ruby selected General Physician as her speciality. General Physician/General

Practitioner, commonly referred to as a medical doctor who specialises in various diseases that affect the body, whose primary treatment does not involve surgery.

For Dr. Ruby to progress with her studies as GP, she had to undergo a lot of practice at her local Hospital in Bulawayo which was the Central Hospital for that City. She also had to do her research programs in the Urban and Rural/Village areas, because the practice was based on research. This was a requirement to pass her PHD Thesis.

The research programs involved - Mortality and Morbidity Rates. Mortality rate refers to the measure of occurrences of death in a defined population during a specified interval. Morbidity rate refers to the percentage of people who have complications from a medical condition, medical treatment or after a medical procedure, calculated the same as in mortality rate.

The reason why Dr. Ruby had to do this research in the Urban and Rural/ Village areas, was to compare the results at the end of the program, which in turn, could be used to make changes or improvements in the Health Sector.

DOCTOR (DR.) RUBY'S WORKFORCE TEAM

Dr. Ruby worked with a team of five registered general nurses (RGN) to support her in her PHD thesis in the research program. She appointed Clara May, one of the RGNs in her team, to lead the group. Clara was appointed to lead the group because she had intensive and extensive experience working in hospitals and clinics in and around Bulawayo. She had very good leadership skills. Clara worked with Dr. Ruby during her holidays only because she was at the time working at Mpilo Hospital in Bulawayo City and was employed on full time basis. Clara had worked in most of the hospitals and clinics where Dr. Ruby's RESEARCH PROGRAMME was based, so she was of great advantage to the research. Dr. Ruby remained the overall head of the group because she was responsible for her PHD thesis accomplishment.

The research program was very challenging but interesting in a way. The team supported Dr. Ruby throughout her research program. This involved working in several hospitals and clinics in different towns and at different times. It also involved a lot of travelling, which made it interesting by meeting people of different diversities and cultures. Some of the topics covered in the research programme were maternal mortality and morbidity rates as explained earlier, in addition to paediatrics, infant mortality rates, family planning, abortion, and holistic medicine/modern science medicines versus traditional medicine.

For you to understand the intensity, depth and length of Dr. Ruby's studies, I will explain what her studies involved so you can understand what some professionals go through to have the titles they have today.

RESEARCH ON TRADITIONAL MEDICINES

As part of her research, Dr. Ruby had to interview the chief leader of all traditional healers in the country. His name is called Freddie Jacobs. Dr. Ruby had to do this before she could conduct her research in the rural/village sector. Freddie had to authorise her first. Research in this area was mainly to find out how traditional medicine relates to modern science in the medical field. It was also to ascertain how authentic it was regarding dosages, hygiene, storage, shelf life, and safety regulations.

Acknowledging that this could be a sensitive issue, Dr. Ruby called for a debriefing with her team of five RGNs (nurses) before entering Freddie's house. They recapped the risk assessments. It was apparent that most members of the group were not keen to interview Freddie.

They voiced their fears in respect that they did not know how much knowledge and power Freddie had when using his herbs (traditional methods) and how much risk it was to them. Clara suggested to meet with Freddie outside in the garden, which he refused. So they were obliged to meet with him in his house. Clara had another clever suggestion, to have lesser people enter the house so that he would not feel overwhelmed with the crowd. Also those who would enter the house to spend as minimal time as possible, just to be on the safe side. To the relief of the rest of the group, only the leaders opted to go inside, that is Dr. Ruby and Clara, as they happened to be the tough ones also. The other four nurses remained in the car.

Dr. Ruby tried to maintain a relaxed atmosphere as much as possible while she interviewed the traditional healer Freddie. Tensions started rising as Freddie was so reserved that it was difficult to extract any valid information from him. He avoided tricky questions to keep his practice safe. The interior of his house appeared scary as it had unusual ornaments and interior decorations. It had dim light and appeared crammed. There was too much furniture and clutter which seemed to move in the dim light. This was a sign that fear was gripping them.

The survey was supposed to be simple and straightforward, question-and-answer format. However for some questions, Freddie just remained silent and glared at them with cold eyes. Dr. Ruby remained as professional as she could when it came to asking him questions of a sensitive nature.

With Freddie's cold eyes still glaring at Dr. Ruby and Clara, the two nurses started feeling uncomfortable, dazed and light-headed. They had not taken any alcohol or any drink at all because they had refused when Freddie offered them. From the beginning they had not trusted him. With eye contact gestures between Dr. Ruby and Clara, they signaled each other to wrap it up quickly and vacate the place. So they wrapped it up and ended the questionnaire. Freddie authorised them to proceed with the research. They shook hands with him and bade him farewell. He said something they did not quite understand. Due to the fact that they wanted to vacate the place quickly they did not bother to ask him, they left the house.

When they were outside, Clara asked Ruby what Freddie had said when they bade him farewell, but Dr. Ruby also could not figure it out. They repeated over and over the phrase Freddie had used, trying to make some sense out of it. They found it so funny, suddenly they were gripped with a fit of laughter, which was spontaneous and uncontrollable.

They got to the car in that state of laughter to meet the rest of the team. The team was shocked to find them in that state because they were the most professional, most thorough, and duty-conscious people they knew, who did not mix business with pleasure. They thought that Dr. Ruby and Clara were obviously drunk, but in fact, they were not. Dr. Ruby and Clara acknowledged that they were under a spell of some sort from Freddie, so Dr. Ruby asked the driver to drive quickly away from the premises of the house. In the car, Dr. Ruby and Clara continued to say the meaningless phrase that Freddie had uttered to them, and this was followed by a fit of laughter. They came to a clearing in the forest as they drove back to their hotel and stopped the car. They all got out and had a breath of fresh air and a cool breeze. The cool breeze seemed to clear their minds, and they came to their senses again as the laughter tapered off. This was a memorable event throughout their practical sessions till the end of the thesis.

This is just to cap on some of the highlights of the dangerous escapades the team encountered in their expedition to support Dr. Ruby with her PHD thesis.

Dr. Ruby did a lot of STATISTICS compiling as part of the studies. Statistics is the science of collecting and analysing numerical data in large quantities, especially for the purpose of inferring proportions in a whole from those in a representative sample.

For this purpose, she hired Andrew Mayo, a student at Bulawayo University studying statistics. Andrew was in his final year of studies at the same university as Dr. Ruby, so they teamed up well. Dr. Ruby had to hire Andrew because compiling statistics is a complex subject for someone who is not trained. So for most of the journeys, he would accompany the team, and at the end of the day, he would compile the statistics. The rest of the team would compile the data and meticulous record-keeping was a requirement. Dr. Ruby and Clara remained professional and articulate as the supervisory bodies of the entire team. The team remained subordinate to Dr. Ruby throughout her studies.

DR. RUBY TRAINS JUNIOR DOCTORS

Dr. Ruby completed her studies at the scheduled time and her PHD Thesis was a success in her speciality as GP. It took her three years to complete this stage. Which makes it a total of twelve years of studying since she completed O-Level.

Fortunately Dr. Ruby got a job abroad which met her specifications. The job was at a Hospital in London. Unfortunately she had to do a Foundation Course for two years because she was coming from a different country. This was a requirement before making progress in any medical speciality. She did the foundation course for two years after which she completed. Now Dr. Ruby had made a total of fourteen years studying period since she separated with Trey. During the entire studying period, she was earning a salary not much different from a student Doctor and which is almost equivalent a senior Registered Nurse.

Dr. Ruby worked a further two years at the hospital to gain more experience before she considered teaching Medical Students. It adds up to sixteen years before acquiring the necessary studies and experience for her chosen speciality. Dr. Ruby got the job she was interested in, training junior doctors in a collage in London.

RUBY'S TITLE CHANGES TO PROFESSOR - PROF

Dr. Ruby worked as a Tutor Doctor, training junior doctors and continued to work at the London hospital for four years. Due to the intensive training, lengthy experience and diligence in business, she was presented with the Honorary Professor Title. She got this title after twenty years of rigorous training and experience. This is from the time she completed O-Levels and went separate ways with Trey. From now on I will address Ruby as Professor Ruby or Prof Ruby.

Prof Ruby though diligent in the business, found her new role as Professor training junior doctors, and working at the hospital, demanding and very busy a schedule. At first, she was overjoyed by becoming a professor as it was one of the highest ranks anyone could reach. After a few years, she found her two roles, as a professor training doctors and working at the hospital become even more busier and exerting pressure on her. It was difficult for her to accomplish the day-to-day tasks without burning out her resilience. Overall, she did not find contentment in her job. The salary was good but not worthy the pressure so she dropped work at the Hospital and maintained teaching medical doctors. This managed to reduce her hours of work but it also reduced her salary, which she did not mind at this stage.

A HIGH RANK IN A JOB IS NOT ALL THAT MATTERS

Prof Ruby acknowledged that it was not just a high-ranking job that mattered in life. She felt that there was something missing, like a missing link, in her life. One would think that a woman of such a high status in life and intelligent, would be one of the happiest people. But no. She was unhappy; something still seemed to lack somewhere.

> Ever learning but never able to come to the KNOWLEDGE of the TRUTH. (2 Timothy 3:7)

Prof Ruby, now in her early thirties, had turned down a good number of men who wanted a meaningful relationship with her. The reason she turned them down was that they did not reach her status quo or something equivalent. Now she felt really lonely after a busy work schedule; she needed someone to chat with, watch a movie, have children, have fun and help with some chores around the house regardless of their status. Prof Ruby found her life boring. She realised she needed a companion, a soulmate to share life with.

She was fortunate enough that after a few years on, she found a man who wanted a meaningful relationship with her. She soon got married to him. He was a medical receptionist by the name of James Jones. They appeared happy together and later were blessed with a son and a daughter, namely Moses and Samantha. Initially, this seemed to be the filling of the seemingly missing link.

Prof Ruby's marriage and the children brought temporary joy to the family. It was apparent that family life brought back the pressure to her schedule. Her life now became hectic, helter-skelter. Prof Ruby was burnt out with work as a lecturer for the medical students, the married life chores, childminding, and the usual household chores. They had a child-minder, but still the pressure of work was pressing on. Though she had long stopped work at the hospital to reduce her hours of work it seemed to benefit her before marriage but not after.

PROFESSOR RUBY IS STRESSED

James Jones Prof Ruby's husband, was a loving husband who always helped whenever he could, but as a medical receptionist, he did not earn much salary. His salary was less than the nurses salary. He also had a busy work schedule. They often had misunderstandings and quarrels. Usually they did not have time for themselves to enjoy life due to their ever busy schedules. The other challenge was that their scope of logical reasoning and solving complex issues in their home differed. This brought conflict in the home. Prof Ruby got stressed up so much that it affected her health and she had to seek medical advice.

Professor Ruby and James could afford a simple holiday a year, live in an average good home, drive average good cars, and pay all their bills monthly. That was what their rigid salaries permitted.

They could not afford luxuries. Prof Ruby had long stopped working at the hospital but it did not benefit her now due to the marriage overload and some financial constraints. They had one source of income each, paid by the company on a specific date each month. They had no control over their salaries, which were disproportional to the workload. Regardless of their hectic schedules, they were paid according to standard rigid salary scales that were determined by the position and experience one had. They were not paid for working overtime.

The general public always think that professors are the highest-paid people in the UK because of their education, but that is not so. People like chief executives (C.E.Os), managing directors, and senior officials, some who hold no formal qualifications, happen to be the highest-paid individuals in the UK. Second to them are the aircraft pilots and flight engineers. These require certain levels of high qualifications. Then in the third place comes the healthcare or medical practitioners, including the medical professors. This group has the most educated, longest, most intense training periods of degree level and above. Unfortunately they are paid the least in comparison to the two groups mentioned above. This third group is the group that Prof Ruby belonged.

MEDICAL CONDITIONS DUE TO STRESS

The busy lifestyle continued to have its toll on Prof Ruby's physical body. Initially when she went to seek medical advice, she received counselling as management of the first signs of stress. The stress degenerated to some medical conditions. She was diagnosed with hypertension (raised blood pressure), depression, asthma and commenced on treatment for all the conditions mentioned above. At one time Prof Ruby had a drug interaction from the medications she was taking. This exacerbated her conditions and delayed control of the conditions despite the fact that she was a medical doctor herself.

James did his best to support his wife, Prof Ruby, with household chores, with the children's chores, and with school runs whenever he could. Soon he was also feeling the pressure and burnt out. He started coming home late from work and spending more time with his friends. Instead of the financial situation getting better because two of them were working and earning salaries, things seemed to get worse. They quarreled a lot. James could not do extra work elsewhere to earn more money because the kids were very demanding and time-consuming. Bringing up children proved to be quite exquisite and expensive also. This only added more stress to Prof Ruby, who was already under a lot of stress. The stress became chronic, meaning the stress was continuous and there all the time.

The stress took its toll on Prof Ruby, and her existing medical conditions EXACERBATED so much that she ended up with cerebral vascular accident (CVA), which in simpler terms is called STROKE. She ended up in the high-dependency unit fighting for her life. By the grace of God, she survived it, and her husband was by her side throughout the illness. She had acute on chronic, meaning she had a sudden onset of a severe condition (stroke) on an existing long-term condition, which is (hypertention). She had to reduce her hours in training doctors due to medical conditions.

Stress can be that bad, so do not overlook the first signs and symptoms of it. It needs medical intervention before it complicates.

REFLECTION ON PROFESSOR RUBY'S LIFE

Reflecting on Prof Ruby's life, she lived a life most women admired—with a high-ranking and good job, intelligent, with a husband and children—and some wished they were in her place. Little did they know that she was stressed up and on treatment. Her salary was not equivalent to her title because of the reduced hours. She was not contented with her life. Her husband was also getting affected by it all and was beginning to lose it.

Such an INTELLIGENT woman as Prof RUBY should have been one of the happiest people in life, but she happened to be stressed with no contentment in life. WHY? One would ask.

The answer is that she was missing an IMPORTANT ELEMENT that is the CATALYST to CATAPULT her life into SUPERABUNDANCE and JOY unspeakable. HOW is this possible? This will be explained in the following chapters after we look at the life of Trey Thomas. So pay attention to details so that you do not miss the important cues and clues.

Chapter 2

TREY THOMAS'S LIFE EXPLAINED/
THE MONEY CODE

If you follow this LINE by LINE, PRECEPT by PRECEPT, you will not miss that CATALYST in the 3D. It is important for me to give practical examples of fictitious people so that when we go deeper in the FATHOMLESS explanations, it will help you understand how to get wealthy (RICH). This is the wealth anyone can get, in other words, RICHES WITHIN YOUR REACH. Know the money CODE and how to DECODE it as you read on.

TREY'S EDUCATION

Now let us look at the life of Trey from the time he did not do well in GCE O-Levels examinations. He went separate ways with Ruby who succeeded at this level. Just to make you understand better, it is hard to find any meaningful job or get enrolled to any college when you do not succeed in the GCE O-Levels. It is considered as the basic or ordinary level you need to pass before proceeding to find any job or enrolling with a college.

TREY'S MINDSET AND VISION

Trey did not consider his not doing well in academics as a failure in life. He knew that he was capable of doing something better and that there was always a way out. He was aware of the great saying that stated that 'EVERY FAILURE BRINGS WITH IT AN EQUIVALENT POTENTIAL SUCCESS'. There was a driving force inside him. So Trey put his mind to work and thought positively always regardless of negative situations. He was aware that there are people known as school drop- outs who rose to great heights, to manage space missions involved in rocket launching and are now Billionaires. On that note he came up with a wise idea.

At this time, Trey had relocated to England, in the United Kingdom, and lived with his friend by the name of Matt Schmitz. Matt was an established businessman trading in electrical goods. He owned a shop in Slough, where his business was doing well, and he was the manager of this shop called Zett- Electrics. Trey assisted his friend Matt to run the shop while he had this wise idea impregnated in his mind - he DESIRED to have his own shop. To be an independent business owner (IBO)—yes, that was his idea and VISION.

As he continued to assist his friend in the shop, Trey paid attention to all the details—running the shop, ordering new equipment, sales, stock control, and managing staff. The more Trey worked in the shop, the more he believed that he could do it. Soon his desire became a BURNING DESIRE with the 'I CAN DO IT' mentality. He did not give room to any doubt regardless of how bleak the situation and circumstances of starting his own business appeared.

TREY'S BURNING DESIRE

Trey's IDEA coupled with the BURNING DESIRE soon gave birth. After a few years working with Matt, Trey started shipping some second-hand and new goods to Harare, his home town. Most people looked down on him as this job was usually considered low rating by many.

More so because they knew him as a school drop-out. Trey was not perturbed by the negative comments and responses. Some were saying, "Going to the UK and coming back to sell us the Rich-man's rubbish". He took it as CONSTRUCTIVE FEEDBACK and he considered improving the quality of his goods. This gave him strength to PUSH ON- Persist Until Something Happens- (PUSH).

> He understood that where there is a VISION, there is a PROVISION by nature itself. This is used more in the Christian faith, where Christians believe that God makes the provision and that he fulfills the desires of your heart (Psalm 37:4).

Second-hand electrical goods are cheap in the UK because most of them are dumped by householders even when they are still in good working order, because they go for newer models on the market. Matt supported Trey a lot in marketing merchandise and checking the goods for safety and good working condition before exporting them to Harare.

Trey continued to work with Matt for a few years while he was learning all the aspects of business and at the same time exporting goods to Harare. Matt was well experienced in managing his electric shop in Slough, the Zett- Electrics situated in the outskirts of London. The goods Trey was exporting consisted of, mainly second-hand electrical appliances in good working order. These comprised of fridges, freezers, fridge-freezers, radios, televisions, stoves, hotplates, irons, vacuum cleaners, dishwashers as the main goods. He also traded in desktop computers, laptops, iPads and others.

Trey did not start the business with all the listed items at once. He started with fewer items then increased gradually the quantities and varieties of items he purchased. He started a small shop in Slough, where he replicated Matt's business skills and acknowledged that it works. The more the local shop was successful for him, the more he increased the goods he sent to Harare. He was assisted by two of his relatives to work in the Slough shop.

Trey noted that this was a lucrative business in Slough, and he considered that this business could do much more for him in Harare. Without wasting much time, he embarked on the idea and put it into motion by purchasing his own shop in Harare. Initially he was selling his goods from his house in Harare.

TREY'S BUSINESS IN HARARE

Trey had started off by doing all sales from his home in Harare because he started with fewer goods. Now he was managing to send more items to his home town, Harare. That was how he managed to purchase a small shop in the outskirts of Harare for his own sales. For this business to be established, he had to make more frequent visits to Harare while he continued to run the shop in Slough also. In Harare, he hired one unemployed electrician to assist in testing his goods for quality and compliance. The electrician helped with the sales also. Trey spent more of his time in Slough UK, than in his small shop in Harare. He continued to buy electrical goods then shipped them to his shop in Harare. He maintained good alliance with his friend Matt. Eventually as the years went by, Trey was sending large quantities of goods to Harare.

Trey's business in Harare progressed well and at a reasonable rate because the market was larger there as compared to the one in Slough. After some years he acquired a bigger shop in the upmarket, in the city centre of Harare. He named this shop the Rising Star. He could see himself rising to great heights in business with no limitations. In no time, he employed trainee and qualified staff as engineers, mechanics, and electricians, as APPRENTICES. The staff would check and fix all the goods to ensure safety and excellent working conditions and PAT tested before selling. In so doing, Trey was also gaining knowledge from his staff as he worked with them.

Trey managed to find trainee engineers and paid them reasonably low rates because most of them were students and there was a high rate of unemployment in the country. The country's political and economic state was in a crisis.

The high percentage of unemployment, acted as an advantage to Trey as he could employ and pay workers at lower rates. These employees did not mind less because half a loaf as better than nothing. At the same time, they were getting on the job training and experience they needed. This in turn, would enable them to obtain job references when the need arose. He had a reasonable number of staff which comprised of sales personnel, a receptionist, and security.

Trey's office comprised of a reception area in the front, a large space to display his goods for sale, an office and another inner office as his own office, a tea room, and toilets. There was a warehouse at the back where some of the goods were stored, checked, fixed, and tested before they were deemed ready for sale.

Most of his goods were in good condition and durable because his staff had good business skills and did their job well. The prices were a mark below all other retail shops because Trey got them quite cheap. This attracted many customers to his shop. He became popular, and he prospered gradually. Trey had a way with customers which just attracted them to him and his businesses. His countenance was ever cheerful. He respected all his customers and staff, and they respected him also. His communication with his customers and staff was professional. He was good-looking and dressed smart for his job. Trey did not mix business with pleasure as most young and good-looking guys would do when surrounded by beautiful women. He focused on improving his business and on expanding it. He knew playing around with women was a distraction to his focus.

TREY'S FAMILY

Trey Thomas got married to a beautiful, loving woman and they had four children. His wife's name was Diana Thomas. His four children comprised of two daughters and two sons. The two sons' names were Joshua and Caleb, and the two daughters, Sophia and April. He bought a house in an exclusive suburb in the low-density area of Harare City called Mount Pleasant. Trey was now living the good, happy life. He had several cars and trucks for himself; for his wife, Diana; and for his business. His shop, the Rising Star, in Harare was packed with goods nicely displayed in an attractive manner and easy for customers to find what they were looking for. The Rising Star shop was ever busy with shoppers attracted by the good quality of the products and competitive prices. Trey was happy and contented as a successful businessman and also as a family man. His wife Diana, and his four children were all happy and contented with his success. It was evident for all to see that he was making good progress in life.

HOUSING BUSINESS IN THE UK

Money continued to flow in and to accumulate in the Rising Star in Harare, the shop owned by Trey Thomas. As he prospered, he came up with another wise idea. His merchandise for his electrical shop in the UK was not doing so well anymore. British people do not go for second-hand goods; they are the ones who give away the goods, and foreigners go for them. His friend Matt was doing well because he was selling new goods only. So Trey supplanted this business with something different. He had another bright idea impregnated in his mind.

The idea that was impregnated in his mind this time was to start HOUSING BUSINESS in the UK. This comprised of buying houses and flats then rent them out. He started by buying one house and renting it out. He increased gradually and steadily as the years went by. With determination and hard work, this business started to pay off. As money started to come in he bought more houses and flats to rent out. Soon he was financially sound as money continued to flow into his businesses. The housing business in the UK, Trey maintained the same trade name for his businesses --the Rising Star.

The electrical shop in Harare, the Rising Star, continued to run and make even more money for him. Trey continued to travel to Harare to manage the businesses, though he could now afford business acquaintances to receive the exported goods for his shop and manage in his absence.

HOUSING BUSINESS IN HARARE

Trey's business, buying and renting out houses in the UK was doing very well and did not demand much input from him as his other businesses in other words it had LOW OVERHEAD. He replicated this business in Harare. To get this business established in Harare, he now spent more time in Harare. Trey had acquired skills in business management and managing staff by experience, in other words, on-the-job training and from his friend Matt and from his shop in Harare. He had prospered in Harare so much that he was now in the same circle as other prominent businessmen.

He had enough money to buy and rent out houses because money was coming from his two electrical shops and housing business on a continual basis. In good time, he owned many houses and flats in Harare, which he was renting out. He found this a more lucrative business with less labour for him because he used the estate agents to manage this business for him. It proved to have low overhead which was of great advantage to him. He planned his businesses well so that he never got overwhelmed. In good course, that is after a few years money started flowing steadily into this businesses, in increasing quantities on a continual basis and from multiple sources.

The more money flowed into Trey Thomas businesses, the more ideas came to his mind, and he endeavoured to make even more money. He was in high spirits and excited and wanted to venture into new frontiers. The idea that came to his mind this time was to start a CLOTHING SHOP. He would dedicate this to his wife, Diana Thomas, would love to manage such a business. It would comprise of buying and selling clothes.

Diana, Trey's wife was a Primary School Teacher. She was working few hours only because she was committed to promoting the upbringing of her children. Caring for four children is a cumbersome task however she had planned it well. The time the children were at school is the time she would be teaching. She would be home before the children completed their lessons. Trey would pick the children when they completed and take them home because he had a flexible routine. He usually went to the UK businesses when the children were on holiday. His home was as well organised as his businesses.

THE CLOTHING SHOP IN HARARE

As Trey continued to prosper, he wasted no time implementing the idea that came to his mind. He had developed a thought process and thought pathway that he followed with each idea that came to his mind. That was why he was quick to process his ideas into the thought pathway and implement the thoughts into their physical equivalent. This was a new and different business that comprised of buying and selling CLOTHES. Trey rented another shop in Harare City for this new business. He dedicated this shop to his wife Diana as planned. Diana was overwhelmed with joy just as her husband had imagined. She acquired skills from her husband on business management. Her husband, Trey, assisted her to manage the business until she could stand on her own. She hired two staff to assist her in the new shop so that she could achieve high standards from the beginning so that this, in turn would attract more customers. Her two daughters, Sophia and April, assisted her in the shop when they were on holiday because they were at college. Diana resigned from her teaching job as she was working a few hours only. She dedicated more time to the business especially when it was starting off.

The clothes shop maintained the family business trade name, which was the Rising Star. The shop consisted of all manner of clothes, shoes, bags, jewellery, and perfumes for both ladies and men, as well as children. Most of these clothes were imports from other countries, mainly from the UK. Trey had stayed in the UK long enough to know the cheaper markets, like the ones in Finsbury Park, Shepherd's Bush, Walthamstow, and many others.

Trey's businesses prospered at a fast rate because he was already established in other businesses, and many trusted in him. He became a very popular and rich individual in town. Many people wanted to be associated with him and to learn how he prospered so much in difficult times. Unemployment was on the rise, and most businesses were struggling to make it. Bearing in mind the fact that some people knew him as school drop out.

TREY'S MINDSET

As more people came to ask Trey about his businesses, another idea came to his mind. Questions and comments, whether positive or negative, he acknowledged them all and recorded them.

Many people would feel interrupted, distracted and delayed by these many questions and comments, but not Trey. He considered them as CONSTRUCTIVE FEEDBACK. He would analyse (ASSESS) them, come up with PLAN OF ACTION, after identifying areas that needed improvement. He would IMPLEMENT as appropriate and EVALUATE in due course. So in actual fact the people actually helped him to improve his businesses. Each time his mind worked this way, he would come up with an idea. It looked like ideas came continually to his mind like a stream of water. His mind was focused on success and expanding business. He never entertained the idea of starting a business and failing. The idea that came to Trey's mind again gave birth. This idea was to construct a PRIVATE BUSINESS MANAGEMENT COLLEGE where he could sell his ideas for money instead of giving them away for free to those that came with many questions.

Yes, ideas can be sold even where merchandise cannot be sold. There is no standard price for ideas because the creator of ideas makes his own price as he deems fit. Not many people know this except those with a different mindset—the mindset of seeing THE RICHES WITHIN YOUR REACH. 'Nothing for nothing' as the saying goes. With this new college, Trey also had the idea that he would find ways of converting listeners into buyers. The buyers would be his own students from the college and many others from various avenues. They would buy his ideas with real money, that is, when they enrol at this college and pay college fees. They could advertise his business when they inform and invite their friends, family, and colleagues to join them at the college. They would also inform them about the goods Trey was selling in his shops.

College students was one way of advertising his businesses, but Trey had several other avenues of advertising his businesses as well. He used his website, social media (like YouTube, LinkedIn, Facebook, Twitter), apps like WhatsApp, scheduled meetings for business promotions and many other avenues.

With a plan of action, Trey implemented the idea and constructed the college he named DIMENSION DISCOVERY DIVISION, simply known as 3D. So people called it 3D College. He welcomed all cadres of pupils and trained them on how to start a business from MEAGRE RESOURCES and progress to a PROFITABLE business and how to be INNOVATIVE. To achieve this, they had to DISCOVER (by searching) a

DIMENSION (extent) above the five senses and separate (DIVISION) themselves from the crowd who cannot think beyond their five senses. This means you deliberately choose to think differently from those people whose minds are confined to the five senses.

MULTIPLE SOURCES OF MONEY ON A CONTINUAL BASIS

Trey had his finances managed at a central base by qualified accountants. Money was flowing in from the two electrical shops, HOUSE/FLATS RENTALS in Slough and in Harare, the CLOTHES SHOP, plus the new business management college in Harare, commonly known as the 3D College, all under the Rising Star, the family business trade name. Six sources of income. He was surely a rising star that kept rising. He was now receiving income, from MULTIPLE SOURCES, in INCREASING QUANTITIES on CONTINUAL BASIS as explained by Napoleon Hill in his book *Think and Grow Rich*. Soon he became a millionaire and expanded in every area of his businesses. He became a very wealthy and popular man. He eventually became a multimillionaire. The same riches that Trey got are WITHIN YOUR REACH.

Trey remained a HEALTHY and WEALTHY man both MENTALLY and PHYSICALLY, and he was a happy and contented man. He started by working very hard and putting a lot of effort. Now he was more relaxed as he had qualified staff to manage and run his businesses.

CHAPTER 3

COINCIDENTAL MEETING/TREY THOMAS AND PROF RUBY SAUNDERS

Coincidentally, Prof Ruby met with Trey in Harare when she was visiting some of her relatives. As explained earlier, Prof Ruby's home town was in Bulawayo, another city which is about four hundred miles from Harare though she now worked in the UK. She was on holiday with her family. She had relatives in Harare.

It was a big surprise for them to meet like this after such a long time. They were both overwhelmed with joy to see how they had both grown to maturity in age. They chatted for a short while before Trey invited her for Lunch the following day which she accepted. Trey was professional and diligent in business, that is why he was quick in thinking and invited Prof Ruby for lunch. He knew there was more to each individual especially this one he knew as the brightest student at school. He was eager to hear a lot more from her.

The following day, Trey and Prof Ruby met for lunch as planned. During the course of the lunch, each of them gave an account of their lives since they completed their academic education and went separate ways. Trey was amazed by how Prof Ruby pursued her career to such heights as Professor but not contented nor happy.

Prof Ruby was also much more amazed that someone she took for a school drop-out had prospered to such heights without much academic education. Trey invited Prof Ruby to take her around his Rising Star business enterprises. They agreed to do this on the next day because they had their lunch in the afternoon and spent all afternoon to the evening chatting. They had not seen each other in more than twenty years.

The next day, Trey met with Prof Ruby as planned for the tour of all the Rising Star Enterprises in Harare. Trey showed Prof Ruby around his businesses starting with the electrical shop, which had grown big and busy. The employees welcomed Prof Ruby with due respect and gave Trey even bigger respect. They were well trained in customer service. Due to his position, employees and customers esteemed Trey very highly. He had a way of dealing with all people, so they could not help liking him and respecting him.

All this amazed Prof Ruby because even though she was a medical professor and many people gave her respect but not this much. In fact, many people challenged her on many occasions as candidates for her position also. Prof Ruby took criticism negatively and was easily offended, hence her frustrations with the job. Trey instead took all criticisms as CONSTRUCTIVE FEEDBACK. He remained cheerful in the middle of criticisms. Trey took down notes mentally and considered every criticism seriously. He used this to make necessary adjustments and changes to his business for improvement. Prof Ruby, on the contrary, met high-profile people of different nationalities who carelessly challenged her position. In her frustrations, she would hit- back negatively. For this kind of response, she lost respect from many people.

They continued going around his Rising Star businesses, from the electrical shop to the CLOTHES shop, which Trey's wife, Diana was managing. It was a great wonder for Prof Ruby to witness the tangible wealth that Trey had accumulated over the years. The shop had state-of-the-art displays of designer clothes. Most of the clothes were imported from the UK, America, and South Africa, and some were locally made clothes. The price range made the clothes affordable to the average-paid people and to the rich, depending on their choice.

The shop was ever busy with shoppers. Diana was well aware that local people preferred imports rather than those made within their country even though they were the same style and the same quality. They liked the foreign designer labels like, Calvin Klein, Ralph Lauren, Christian Dior, Armani, Valentino, Chanel, Gucci, Prada, Givenchy, DKNY, Hugo Boss, and many others. In other words, what most of them went for, were the designer LABELS just to brag, though some were genuinely going for quality.

The housing business Trey showed Prof Ruby electronically as this covered a large area and in different locations in Harare and in the UK. It was better and clearer to view electronically because this allowed 3D images, which in turn allowed a tour of the houses and view inside and out.

Trey saved the best wine for last according to the Bible scripture in John 2:9–10, that is, he showed Prof Ruby his training college last. Trey took Prof Ruby to his 3D College. The building was spectacular with modern-style design and with good and modern-style furniture, computers, and interior decorations. Each room also had a board for electronic demonstrations and presentations. It was weekend, and the college was closed for students, so it was easier for Trey to go around and show Prof Ruby inside the classrooms.

The 3D College had five separate classes for different courses with the capacity of fifteen students per class. The duration of the courses ranged from two weeks to two years depending on various aspects, like the nature of the course, the number of courses, and individual skills, abilities, and capabilities.

Here's an overview of the courses provided at 3D College:

1. Operations and project management—which had two main categories, namely operations strategy and project management
2. Marketing management, public relations and customer relationship management, branding and sales
3. Administrative and secretarial skills

These courses aimed at giving students basic skills in business. The major part of the learning and emphasis was on using the power of your mind. I will not go deeper into what these courses comprised of because I do not want you to derail from the point I am making. It's all about going beyond the five senses and entering into the FAITH DIMENSION. This is explained as you continue to read on.

At this point, an idea came to Prof Ruby's mind, and she made a definite decision. The definite decision that Prof Ruby made and the corresponding action she took will be explained later after we REFLECT on the lives of these two characters, Trey and Prof Ruby. So keep following the illustrations closely so that you do not miss anything. It's like a code: if you miss any figure, letter, word, signal, or symbol, then you will not be able to open that safe or whatever it is that you were trying to DECIPHER. So follow this closely. I have made it simple enough for anyone to understand.

CHAPTER 4

REFLECTING ON THE LIVES OF TREY THOMAS AND PROF RUBY SAUNDERS

Why do you think the one who was doing well in school, utilised her potentials to the fullest, was not contented but the one who was considered a school drop-out was contented, wealthy and healthy?

Prof Ruby, while highly skilled, climbed the ladder in academic and professional education, ranked high in her medical profession, reached the level of a professor, married to a loving husband and with two children, was not happy in life and not contented. Let me use a Bible quote to explain this.

> I returned and saw under the sun, THAT THE RACE IS NOT to the SWIFT, nor the battle to the strong, neither yet bread to the wise, nor yet RICHES to the man of understanding, nor yet favour to men of SKILL; but time and chance happens to them all. (Ecclesiastes 9:11 KJV)

The above verse explains that it is not enough to be wise and skilled for one to prosper and be happy in life. Like the saying

'Knowledge is Power', this is not always correct because knowledge does not attract money. It is only potential power. It takes much more than that. You have to journey through a pathway of IDEAS, ASSESSMENT, PLANNING, IMPLEMENTATION AND EVALUATION as explained earlier, which in itself explain how to use that knowledge after you acquire it. For we know that hard work and honesty will not bring you riches. Riches respond to definite commands and demands based on definite principles. Don't get me wrong, I am not advising you to be dishonest neither I am despising academic knowledge and wisdom. It is the principle thing that we all need to form the basis for all our achievements. You only need to add something more to it.

> Wisdom is the principle thing; therefore get wisdom: and with all thy getting get understanding. (Proverbs 4:7 KJV)

The verse above makes it clear that it is vital to get wisdom, and with it, you need to get the understanding also. There is no looking down on skilled people. There are only a few things they miss to live a contented life. This group of people will find it easier to follow the few steps explained in the following chapters.

TREY'S LIFE—THE DIMENSIONS EXPLAINED

The gateway to success is explained as we take a closer look at the DIMENSIONS. It explains how anyone can lay hands on the riches they desire in life. These are the RICHES WITHIN YOUR REACH. In it is the CODE, and how to DECODE it is all explained in detail.

It may not be put on a platter for you to see this is the code and how to decode it. That is why you need the patience to read every line carefully so you can catch it and not miss it. Like being given a map to find the hidden treasure, it will not be as easy as ABC. All it takes is vigilance in studying the map and the clues surrounding it and patience in searching, then you will surely find the hidden treasure. So likewise, you need to pay attention to details and not skip some pages to try to get to the code. By decoding this way, you will miss it, for it does not work that way. Try not to speed read, take your time, focus, ingest it, ruminate and digest it. It might change your life forever.

CHAPTER 5

THE FAITH DIMENSION

We have reflected on the life of Trey. Now I am going to uncover the key elements that catapulted him into prosperity. Trey did not take his drop-out from school as a failure in life. It was not the end of the world to him. He was broad-minded. He operated by a different set of rules. He was success-conscious. In other words, he had a MINDSET of saying NO to failure or defeat.

Trey believed in MAINTAINING A POSITIVE ATTITUDE despite the attributes of this world. He lived above the elements of this world. The driving force behind his belief system can be described by one word—FAITH. Faith eradicates limitations and is THE FORCE that drives true Christians into performing TRUE MIRACLES.

To the surprise of many, FAITH does not only work for Christians. It works for non-Christians just as good as it does for Christians. It all depends on your belief system, how you understand it, and how you make use of it. FAITH IS THE DIMENSION ABOVE THE FIVE SENSES.

What are the FIVE SENSES?

All human beings are known to have five senses, as follows:

1. Sense of SIGHT, which is known as visual perception.

2. Sense of HEARING, which is known as auditory.
3. Sense of SMELL, which is known as olfactory.
4. Sense of TASTE, which is known as gustatory.
5. Sense of TOUCH, which is known as tactile.

Some people are known to have THE EXTRASENSORY PERCEPTION, which is the SIXTH sense. It is the faculty of perceiving things by means of telepathy. It is also known as INSPIRATION or message—MESSAGE from that which is derived from INFINITE INTELLIGENCE. Christians simply call it FAITH.

There is also the vestibular sense, which is body balance, rotation, and gravitation, and proprioception (perception) sense, which is for position, motion, and equilibrium. These last two senses are less referred to in general terms because they are often used in medical science and by healthcare professionals.

Let's look at a scriptural verse.

> Now FAITH is the substance of things hoped for, the evidence of things not seen. (Hebrews 11:1 NKJV)

The scripture above explains what faith is. Faith is that sixth dimension that you can activate and enter in and live in. (Sixth dimension which is the sixth sense. Some want to classify it as the fourth dimension which comes after the three dimensional world). All this does not matter the faith definition is the same. In the FAITH DIMENSION - you desire in your mind, see the picture, define it, making clear what you DESIRE in life. Have hope that you will get it. This kind of hope is not a mere hope that maybe I will get it or maybe not. It is definite.

This is the faith that the desire in your mind, for a project or business is definite. With that imagination, you get your hands on it, grasp it, and possess it. You get the evidence (proof) in your mind that you now own it and there is no room for doubt. You maintain the faith until your actions become a conviction that you have possessed it. You remain focused on the business this way without wavering till it is deposited and registered in your conscious mind.

When information is registered in the conscious mind, it will then be transferred into the SUBCONSCIOUS MIND. The SUBCONSCIOUS MIND will capture the line of thought you are presenting it with and picture the project (business) you are visualising is stored. This will subsequently be transmitted into intelligence. The intelligence compels your body to act on it appropriately.

Hence, the joyful countenance of Trey. Trey could see success already because his mind was seeing business positively. He could see himself buying and selling electrical goods. He saw success only, and it was so evident and convincing in his mind that he saw himself rising to the heights of prosperity. It tallies with the saying, 'where there is LIFE, there is HOPE' and 'Where there is a WILL, there is a WAY'. Trey understood the fact that THE ONLY LIMITATION IS THAT WHICH ONE SETS UP IN HIS OWN MIND. There is no limit to how rich you can get. The sky is the limit as some put it, but the sky is limitless. So ironically they are actually saying there is no limit.

Trey believed that, EVERY ELEMENT OF FAILURE EMBEDDED IN ITSELF IS ALSO AN EQUIVALENT ELEMENT OF SUCCESS.

> This tallies with the scriptural verse in 1 Corinthians
> 10:13 NIV:
> No temptation has overtaken you except what is
> common to mankind. And God is faithful; HE WILL
> NOT LET YOU BE TEMPTED BEYOND WHAT YOU CAN

BEAR. But when you are tempted, HE WILL PROVIDE A WAY OUT so you can endure it.

How it works is that you do not take any CHALLENGE as a deterrent or failure but rather as STEPPING STONES TO YOUR VICTORY. Do not address the problem but rather look for its SOLUTION. Do not blame people for disappointing you, have the SYSTEM THINKING which means something in the system needs you to FIX it. As we observed earlier, every problem comes packaged with its own solution, that is, transmuting your problems or failures into dreams of a CONSTRUCTIVE NATURE.

PROF RUBY'S IDEA

When Trey took Prof Ruby round his business enterprises, the RISING STAR, she had an idea that came to her mind. I mentioned earlier that I will explain her idea later on, it is now explained. Ruby noted that Trey rose to heights in business from humble beginnings. Considering what she saw during the tour of the Rising Star enterprises Prof Ruby was humbled. Despite being a medical professor she opted to learn something from the 3D college. She realised she was missing an element to boost her finances. There is a saying, 'It is the small things that matter in life'. No matter who you are or where you are, missing the small elements in life will affect your entire life. She made up her mind enrolled at the 3D college for a two weeks course. Ruby was intelligent and quick to learn so two weeks was adequate for her to learn and grasp the concept before she flew back to the UK.

In the two weeks that Ruby enrolled at the 3D college, she managed to grasp the concept, which is the element that was missing to catapult her into superabundance. She learnt that one source of money on fixed bases can never be adequate regardless of who you are. It is like one going for national service, in other words you are not really doing it to benefit yourself and your family but to benefit the nation. That is how she now perceived working for the government is like. Some put it this way- do not put all your eggs in one basket. Meaning it is risky and has limitations.

Prof Ruby flew back to the UK with her family. She and her husband James started working on the key elements, assessing, planning, implementing and evaluating using the power of the mind above the six senses - FAITH. They followed all the steps of FAITH DIMENSION as will be explained in the next chapters. It took a good number of years for Prof Ruby and her husband working with the right mind- set, coupled with her existing intelligence to manage to save money for a new business. They considered HOUSING business has this has LOW OVERHEAD. They did not find the capital to start the business as a challenge any more but as a drive. They worked in unison with each other and managed to have enough resources for depositing a house to let. They were guided by Trey how to manage this business from the start. With the positive mind-set and determination they made good progress in this area. Over the period they purchased more houses to let and this made a lot of difference to their income.

Ruby adhered closely to all the aspects of business she had learnt at the 3D college. Her husband James also grasped the idea. It is not all about learning, it is about applying the principles to attract money. You can be learning half of your life or all your life while someone without much learning starts making money while you are still learning. By the time you complete your studies the one who started applying principles that attract money, would have well established businesses and has made tremendous progress and has prospered already.

Trey reduced the hours he was working as a medical receptionist when the money started flowing steadily in the business. The receptionist job was a very busy job for little benefit. He concentrated more on the expanding business and taking care of his family. He benefited more in doing this because it brought more peace in the home. After some years they ended up with many houses and flats they were renting out.

Now they were enjoying wealth coming from MULTIPLE SOURCES, in INCREASING QUANTITIES on CONTINUAL BASIS. They hired Estate Agents to manage their properties which lessened the workload for them. Some luxuries were now affordable, despite the reduced hours of work in the healthcare sector. Their income was now enough to meet their needs and extra for saving. Prof Ruby now had peace of mind at work and people duly respected her as she adhered to all the aspects of training she received at the 3D college. The results were evidently positive. She was not getting burnt out any more because her husband had more time for the kids and home affairs. In fact they both had more time to spend with the children and could now afford some luxuries. They became a happy family. Prof Ruby's medical conditions and stress subsided gradually over the time until she was stress free. When the underlying problem-STRESS-was eliminated, she soon was taken off medications because she was totally cured. She remembered to thank Trey and wished she had known about this element earlier in life.

It does not matter how much education and skills you have acquired, as long as you have one source of fixed income, you might never get contented with life, there is something you are missing.

There is always more to the intellectual person than the eye can capture nor the mind can perceive. Hence you can always learn something from the very person you look down on. The very things most people consider trivial are usually the things that matter in life.

You cannot imagine how many diseases and conditions are due to stress. Stress comes with a full package of diseases and conditions. Usually the lack of money or spouse is the root cause. Sometimes it is challenges one cannot fix. It is unbelievable that a life of joy, peace and love is what eradicates and prevents most diseases. This is what the creator of humanity wanted it to be in the garden of Eden. That is why every human being wants to be loved and to love someone.

> And now these three things remain: FAITH, HOPE
> AND LOVE. But the greatest of these is LOVE.
>
> (1 Corinthians 13:13 NIV)

These three things mentioned above, are the greatest forces on earth. The greatest of these three being LOVE. The whole chapter of 1 Corinthians 13 describes this love. If you can walk in love according to this chapter, you can conquer and achieve anything in this world.

CHAPTER 6

FAITH DIMENSION PROCESS— EXPLAINED IN ELEVEN STEPS

For one to be a Christian, it's all by FAITH. That is the reason why it is not everybody who believes in Christianity.

The MIND OF MEN is known to be INFLUENCED BY THE GREATEST SINGLE FORCE which is called CHRISTIANITY.

This is not so easy to have faith and process it to work, till your imagination is tangible. The simple steps that follow makes it easier for anyone to understand and to make their faith work.

STEP 1—HAVE AN IDEA (KNOW WHAT YOU WANT)

Be DEFINITE about what you want, which means know exactly what you want. Not just maybe this or maybe that. At first, many ideas will come flooding your mind. You need to ASSESS, screen them and trim them down one by one until you remain with one. If it is a business idea, know exactly what sort of business you want. Trey wanted to buy and sell second hand electrical goods, that is what he could afford at the time. You do the same with whatever idea you have that may differ with what Trey had. Work out how much money you want to put in it and how much you expect to come out of it. You can calculate it as the annual income you desire.

God seems to respond to people who know exactly what they want in life and are determined to get it. An idea is an intangible force which can be converted into material of its equivalent. Ideas are known to have more power than the physical brains, where they originate from. It is an intriguing fact to know that these ideas have the power to live on after the brains that gave birth to them have returned to dust.

We could give reference to the power of Christianity. Christ had an idea to save humanity and guide Christians on how to live their lives on earth. These ideas were written in a book called the Bible. Christ has since died and rose up again and lives again today in us, us in him, he is around us, in heavenly realms and everywhere. This happened more than two thousand years ago, but his IDEA is still alive and marching on to this day. Also I could give reference to the Wright Brothers, Orville and Wilbur in 1903 invented the first powered flight. They have since died but their idea lived on to this day. The flights have since improved, but still it is the Wright Brothers idea that has lived on to this day.

STEP 2—DREAM/IMAGINATION

Have the IMAGINATION/DREAM. Picture this business or whatever thing you want to achieve over and over in your CONSCIOUS MIND. Focus on it, cultivate it, and concentrate on it. Fixate your attention with eyes closed until you can see the positive end result of your business or whatever you chose to work on, in your mind. This idea can become a giant under its own power if you keep nursing it long enough. That is what ideas are like when you give them guidance. They will take on power of their own and eradicate all doubts. To achieve this, you have to choose a time in the day to focus this way. You can choose to do it twice a day, same times each day. The length of time you spent focusing on this dream is your choice, depending on your schedule. You can choose about ten to twenty minutes per day, depending on your preference. See yourself already running the business or that which you chose to focus on. All this will be happening in your mind.

STEP 3—KEEP A RECORD

Keep a record of that which you are seeing in your dream, which means WRITE IT DOWN. You can write down using a pen and paper but preferably keep an electronic record, which can be kept secure. If you do not write down your vision, you may forget some of the important clues that you get. The more you write, you will realise that at first the clues do not articulate. With time, you will notice the clues starting to articulate, like jigsaw puzzle parts getting together and forming a picture. When you see this happen you know you are getting there. Get into the details of your business—how and where to get the materials and what mode of transport you need to transport the materials from one place to where you want them. Find out your market—where to sell and who to sell to. Find the best way to organise your team—who you can work with to achieve your goal. Consider how much money you can afford to start with—what support you get from those who support small businesses starting off. Also, consider the annual income.

The Lord answered me and said, 'Write the vision, and make it plain on tablets, that he may run who reads it.' (Habakkuk 2:2 NKJV)

These were the words of the creator of heaven and earth to Habakkuk. The vision was for an appointed time, so it was important to write the details down so that at the appointed time, all the information would be made available with no missing data or altered information.

In the same way, it is important to write your idea down with all the details. Screen and trim down your information then implement. This way you will not lose valuable information. Nowadays, people store their information on electronic gadgets which keep information safe and secure, easier to edit and to retrieve in due course.

CHAPTER 7

STEP 4—STRONG DESIRE

Have a STRONG DESIRE to convey into possession that which you have written down. This desire is derived from deep inside the imagination in your mind using the thought pathway. This INTANGIBLE DESIRE can be transmuted into a physical one of its equivalent magnitude. Trey was successful because he visualised success in his mind (success-minded) and focused on his strong desire positively and converted it into its physical equivalent. A STRONG DESIRE to attain the goal. Trey persisted and was COMMITTED to achieve his goal, so he pressed on with a pleasant attitude, unperturbed by opposition and those who did not think he could achieve much in life. This was evidenced by their comments and their demeanour, but Trey refused to be discouraged, he remained strong and maintained his commitment to the tasks he laid down for himself. He gave no room for excuses, and he was not doing what was convenient but what it takes to reach his goal. It is never easy, it is self- determination.

Delight yourself in the Lord, and He will give you the DESIRES of your heart. (PSALM 37:4 KJV)

This verse shows that where there is DESIRE, a PROVISION -SUPPLY will be made available, in this case, by the Lord God himself.

However, even if you do not believe in God but have a strong desire long enough, it will soon be converted to its physical equivalent. How? you may ask. It means a tangible provision will be made by NATURE itself.

STEP 5—MEDITATE

Meditate all steps from step 1. Focus on that which you have written down. To meditate is to focus on the thing you want to achieve in deep thought. You do not allow any other thought to distract or derail you from the focal point. To achieve that, you choose a quiet room. You start silently, then after a while, you start to speak it out softly, like whispering. Maintain focus on and that which you want to achieve.

Keep your thoughts focused while you are whispering. Consider when to start the business, how to start it, how to achieve it and then possess it. This process is called PLANNING MENTALLY. On this step, usually nobody acknowledges what you are doing except you, because it is more effective when done privately. You do not tell your vision to anyone at this stage because if you trust them and tell your vision they might disappoint you. They can steal your vision and implement it well ahead of you. This could be because they they already have resources in place which you might not have at the time.

It is like someone building the foundation of his house. No one will have an idea how exactly his house will look like on completion by just looking at the foundation. The house that takes longer building the foundation is usually the better and more durable house as compared to the one whose foundation is rushed. So take your time with PLANNING MENTALLY and MEDITATION.

STEP 6—PROCLAIM

PROCLAMATION is a clear DECLARATION of that which you have been whispering about. In other words, you are still meditating, but now you are saying it out loud but privately. You are convinced that your mental planning has given birth to a definite, precise way and method of how to go about your planned business or whatever you have been focusing on.

You embrace it; hence, you can boldly say it out loud, like a shout of victory. You can continue to shout this way, in your house, even when you are walking or driving. You are taking possession in utterances. Continue to do this for a considerable time. It looks like crazy but believe me it works. Maintain consistency till you are ready to take the next step.

STEP 7—PERSIST

PERSISTENCE is to continually harness all the steps explained above until it becomes an OBSESSION and the thought that continually preoccupies your mind. You need to go back to all the steps from one to six so you know exactly where you are and what you are doing.

Keep on focusing until the desire to possess the riches become the DOMINATING THOUGHT in your mind. Remain committed and consistent to do whatever it takes to achieve your goals. Remove any doubts or negative thoughts.

You know you are on the right track by your commitment and following the steps without wavering. This is the same PRINCIPLE of PERSISTENCE that Christians use to achieve their goals.

> The heartfelt and PERSISTENT prayer of a righteous
> man [believer] is able to accomplish much [when put
> into action and made effective by God, it is dynamic
> and can have tremendous power]. (James 5:16 AMP)

You do not have to be a Christian, but it is a known fact that if you do and persevere long enough, you will be able to achieve the desired goal.

P.U.S.H - Persist Until Something Happens.

Chapter 8

STEP 8—PLAN/STRATEGISE

PLANNING and STRATEGISING is the next thing you do after following the steps above. Continue to meditate, persisting on that which you desire and what you have written down. When you do this new ideas will come in. These new ideas help in the planning process. The mental planning is now taking form as STRATIGIC PLANNING AND STRATIGIC THINKING.

If you realize that you need more knowledge before implementing your business physically. You can get specialized knowledge on the business you have selected by getting courses on independent business owners offered by libraries at subsidized fees, online learning, attending business promotion meetings, learning from other reliable business owners, and many others. If you already have the skills and are confident enough, you do not need to go through all this.

You shift the information you have in your mind around as new and more intelligent ideas start to come in. Add and subtract information when the ideas that were not quite clear now take up form and become clearer. You start to get precise details on how to run the business. Write down the nature of the business, the date you want to start, the venue for your business, all materials required, the amount of money you can start with (capital), and the amount you expect to get back.

For example, you may say you want to accumulate £50,000,00 in the first year. You must decide that the reward of your business is worthy of the capital and effort you are putting into it.

> For I know the PLANS and THOUGHTS I have for you says the Lord, thoughts and plans for welfare and peace and not for evil, to give you hope in your final outcome. (Jeremiah 29:11 AMP)

This scripture shows us that God, the creator of humanity (human beings), PLANS the life he wants his people to live and encourages them. Likewise, planning is necessary for human beings to achieve their goals. Your plans give you the drive to push on, and they encourage you.

> A man's mind PLANS his way [as he journeys through life], but the Lord directs his steps and establishes them. (Proverbs 16:9 AMP)

The scripture above shows that a man (a human being) is ever planning in his mind whether he is conscious of it or not. He is designed to do so by his creator. That is how important planning and strategizing is, to get direction so that one can establish their businesses.

STEP 9—THE DATABASE

THE SUBCONSCIOUS MIND is that part of the mind that one is not fully aware, and it influences one's actions and feelings. The subconscious mind is fed by information from your conscious mind. It is the DATABASE OF EVERYTHING that ever happened in your life, even your memories, thoughts, and skills. It is ever working day and night. That means it is working even in your sleep. You can have control of what is in your conscious mind, but you do not have much control once the information enters your subconscious mind.

Look at it this way. You have fed your conscious mind with all the eight steps above, and all this information gets stored in the DATABASE, which is your subconscious mind and which you do not have much control of. That is the reason one should always think positively. These are the unseen FORCES OF FAITH which COMPELS you into ACTION. These are the same forces which make true MIRACLES evident to the eyes of the true believer to see.

Bear in mind that whatever you put in your subconscious mind, whether positive or negative or good or evil, will yield you equivalent results. Whether you know it or not, whether you believe it or not, it remains a true fact. Ignorance is not an excuse. For example, when Trey was a school drop-out, if he had believed that he had failed in life, nothing worthwhile would have come out of him in the form of a job or finances. If he had believed in failure and continued that way long enough, he would probably have died without achieving anything in life.

> For the weapons of our warfare are not carnal, but mighty through God to the pulling down of STRONG HOLDS. Casting down IMAGINATIONS and every high thing that exalts itself against the knowledge of God, and bringing into captivity every THOUGHT to the obedience of Christ. (2 Corinthians 10:4–5 AMP)

The scripture above is referred to as THE BATTLEFIELD OF THE MIND by some preachers.

There is so much activity in the mind. We are loading it with information all the time. Like your smart phone or computer, it has a certain specified capacity of information or pictures it can accommodate; otherwise, it runs out of space or slows down in function. It needs regular updating and cleaning up using anti-viruses. The mind of mankind also needs the same clean-up and updating, which it usually does by self-cleaning. In addition to diet, exercises and other activities. You can discard unwanted thoughts as they come to you so that you do not overload your mind with unwanted things or excess baggage. Christians do this by reading the Bible, praying, and worshiping. It replenishes their minds.

This is the reason why in old age the mind gets slow, because it is bunged up with too much information since childhood and is running out of space and needs cleaning up. The thought pathway is interrupted by the ageing process and damaged brain tissue. This leads to conditions like dementia and many other medical conditions.

Chapter 9

STEP 10—IMPLEMENTATION

ACTION TIME! All the steps from 1 to 9 have GIVEN BIRTH. If you keep repeating the processes above in your conscious mind, in due course it offloads all the materials above into your SUBCONSCIOUS MIND and in the right proportions. This becomes a PROPELLING FORCE that COMPELS the individual to ACT ON their DESIRES.

The driving force from within will be so intense that your focus will be on the business project only and putting things into action. Once you start to act on it, you will notice that all the things you planned will fall in place much easier than you ever imagined. However, let us not overlook the fact that in some instances, you might meet challenges here and there. The faith you have built up in you remains your driving force regardless of the setbacks you may encounter in the process of setting your business into locomotion. Once the motion starts, you notice that nothing can stop you from moving forward, so you press onwards towards the mark.

> Now to him that is able to do exceedingly abundantly above all that we ask or think, ACCORDING TO THE POWER THAT IS AT WORK IN US, to him be glory in

the church by Christ Jesus to all generations, forever and ever. Amen. (Ephesians 3:20–21 NKJV)

The power at work is invested in you and in every individual. It takes faith to extract it out. Anyone can do this if vigilant enough to follow all the steps explained above. You need to put effort and determination in the business; in other words, be committed. Have a habit of completing the tasks that you have started. Do not have too many unfinished businesses; it will only slow you down or even confuse you. Be wise, prioritize tasks, confidence in decision-making, flexibility, and prompt to make changes (within the same business) as unprecedented situations arise.

PLEASE NOTE; I explained earlier on, that you do not have to be a Christian for FAITH and all the steps explained above to work for you. This can work for anyone in any business or endeavour, only it will work better for Christians because they believe in their God to bless their businesses, they already understand faith. PRINCIPLES AND FACTS can work for anyone if used in the right proportions and appropriately.

I hope the information elaborated in the STEPS OF FAITH to achieve those riches you desire in your life have been helpful. It will make more sense when you start the motion, then you will acknowledge that the process works. Remember, it does not happen overnight. It's training your mind first to think positively and above the six senses always. Discard emotional baggage and refrain from negative-thinking people.

STEP 11—REFLECTION AND EVALUATION

Now you have implemented your plans into action, and your business has started and is moving forward. Maintain your faith through out the whole process until your business is established. Give yourself a timescale, for evaluating the progress of your business. The time scale varies, three to six months might be palatable for some but others may prefer a year. The timescale will depend on your personal preferences based on the pace of your business. The slower your business is running, the more often you need to evaluate, to identify the cause. Rectify issues at an early stage when you detect them.

You may need to make adjustments here and there as you make progress. The earlier issues are rectified, the better for the business. It has been noted that, issues overlooked from the beginning will have bad repercussions later on your business. The faster your business is running, the lesser times you may need to evaluate, because you are probably on the right track and your business is running according to your plan.

As you make progress in your business, you keep reflecting back on the relevant steps above, maintain your faith and remain positive always despite setbacks. Speak out positive words to yourself to stay strong and to encourage yourself. Let the 'I can do' mentality dominate your thoughts. Focus on the task. This is how you reach your goal. It is never a bed of roses. Most people know this but they get discouraged at some point and give up. Then they lose everything and find someone to blame. It requires self-discipline, determination, commitment, and mental and physical vigilance and resilience.

Chapter 10

IT CAN BE CHOICE TO BE RICH

> Some are born great, some achieve greatness and
> some have greatness thrust upon them.
> —No Fear Shakespeare, *Twelfth Night*, Act 2, Scene
> 5, Page 7/SparkNotes

Since I read Shakespeare's book at school, I have never forgotten this quotation. Which of the three characters referred to by Shakespeare are you? If you're born great or born with greatness thrust upon you, you probably don't need to do much to maintain your greatness, which in other words is wealth or riches. If you are one who achieves greatness, then you are in the group of the characters I explained in my book.

Riches are not meant for certain selected groups of people. It is the know-how that is required. With the right mindset, after reading this book you can change your life. Being financially sound can be a choice. Not a fake millionaire because of weak currencies in your country. In the year 2020 the weakest currency was 1 USD = 42,105 not to mention the country. More than forty two thousand equivalent to just one USD. This means you just need US$ 24 to be a millionaire. There are many countries with weak currencies. Best to rate yourself using the strong currencies. Become millionaire in the currencies that are worthy, like Pound Sterling, United States dollar, Euro, Canadian dollar, Swiss franc and others. Dreams can come true.

Albert Einstein states, 'Insanity is doing the same thing, over and over again, but expecting different results.' This is debatable as some say he never said this. It does not matter where the saying originated from, but the saying remains a fact whether you believe it or not.

If it is not working do not keep doing the same thing, adjust or change the strategy. Faith does not work with doubt, these two contrasts each other. Most peoples faith fail when they consider in their belief system that the task is outside their scope of competence. This shows that the steps were not followed accurately. It has been explained in the chapters above how you can enhance your skills if need be. But as long as there is some doubt in the process, it means you have broken the momentum and you will not achieve desired results. A positive mindset, which accommodates no doubt at all but conviction only will accelerate your momentum and things will work positively for you.

I have made considerable repetition of some phrases and words, this is deliberate, so you know where to put the emphasis. They are the KEY phrases and words to pay special attention to.

Conclusion

If at first you do not understand this book, read it over again. To understand it better, read the whole book and do not select certain chapters; otherwise, the concept may slip through your fingers. I have helped many people with the 'I cannot do this and I cannot do that' mentality. The moment they changed the way they think, they managed to achieve their goals. They had to acquire and to maintain a positive attitude in everything they did to win.

Attitude for altitude. You choose the right attitude for the goal you want to reach. The more positive you are, the higher you will go. The more negative you are, the more you will experience stagnation or even recession in your activities. This does not refer only to the businesses or endeavour you might make; it refers to the attitude you have for the people you meet in your everyday life. When people make achievements in life, are you happy for them? Do you genuinely rejoice with them? Or are you one of those who sulk, envy, and get jealous or even say wicked things?

There is a saying, 'What goes around comes around', meaning you will have to deal with the consequences of your actions at some point in your life.

Some say, 'What you say is what you get', meaning your words have the power to locate you at some point in your course of life.

Hence, let only positive vibe escape your mouth and dominate your mind, unless it is constructive feedback. How wonderful it can be when all your positive vibes come back to you as an exceedingly great reward. It is worthy, and it is a fact, believe it or not. The choice is yours.

> "Listen closely, I have set before you today life and prosperity and death and adversity in that I command you today to love the Lord your God-----". (Deuteronomy 30:15-16 AMP)

May God bless you for reading this book. May your life have a positive change. I would love your comments.

Watch out for forthcoming publications:

1. *How to CHANGE YOUR HUSBAND in a MONTH*
2. *Life as a SINGLE WOMAN / MAN*
3. *SURVIVING The TIMES*

GOALS

S. G. ----SPECIAL GRACE -- WORSHIP GROUP

1. To inspire people from all walks of life understand how to worship God--IN SPIRIT AND IN TRUTH according to GOD'S LOVE AND GRACE.
2. To share my TESTIMONY
3. To share with them some of THE BASIC PRINCIPLES for a SUCCESSFUL LIFE, described in my books.

HOW TO RECEIVE SALVATION

This is also known as TO BE BORN AGAIN

I would like to help someone receive their salvation. It takes about five minutes only to change your destination forever. It is not by your good works as many may think. It has nothing to do with your works. All people are born under the sin committed by Adam in the garden of Eden, whether you do good works or not you would still a sinner before God. We thank God the matter of sin was dealt with.

The law came with Moses from God to keep people from sin but it actually made them sin more and exposed their sins because they were not capable of keeping the law.

God loved all the people he created so much, that despite their sins he sent his only Son Jesus on earth to die for the people.

Jesus knew no sin but he had to die so that he could carry all the sins of the people. When Jesus died on the cross, he carried all the sins of all the people. He was buried. On the third day he arose from the dead and is living in Heavenly places today. His resurrection brought justification to all people. Every person's sins committed in the past, present and in the future are counted on Jesus which means you have been forgiven by God. God sees you as a righteous person. This is the reason you do not need to worry about the works of flesh.

--John 3:16

HOWEVER TO RECEIVE SALVATION YOU HAVE TO BELIEVE THE ABOVE AND CONFESS WITH YOUR MOUTH.

--because if you acknowledge and confess with your mouth THE LORD JESUS and BELIEVE IN YOUR HEART that GOD RAISED HIM from the dead, YOU WILL BE SAVED. (Romans 10:9 AMP)

For with the heart man believes unto righteousness and with the mouth confession is made unto salvation. (Romans 10:10)

AND IT SHALL BE THAT EVERYONE WHO CALLS UPON THE NAME OF THE LORD, SHALL BE SAVED. (Acts 2:21)

Salvation is that simple. You need to BELIEVE the above scriptures first, then open your mouth and say;

"Lord God, I believe with my heart in Jesus Christ, the Son of the Living God. I believe Jesus you died for me and God raised you up from the dead and you live today. I confess with my mouth your Lordship in my life from this day. Through Jesus, I am now born again and I have received salvation. I am now a child of God and have eternal life. Thank you Lord for saving my soul".

CONGRATULATIONS! You now walk in the newness of life, you are a child of God.

You may not feel anything physical because it is all by faith. Only believe.

To continue to grow as a Christian you can contact the details given below.

INDEX

www.ingramcontent.com/pod-product-compliance
Lightning Source LLC
Chambersburg PA
CBHW031152250726
48655CB00002B/938